STREAMS OF HISTORY

THE RENAISSANCE AND REFORMATION

STREAMS OF HISTORY

THE RENAISSANCE AND REFORMATION

BY

ELLWOOD W. KEMP

EDITED BY

LISA M. RIPPERTON

YESTERDAY'S CLASSICS

CHAPEL HILL, NORTH CAROLINA

This edition, first published in 2008 by Yesterday's Classics, an imprint of Yesterday's Classics, LLC, is an edited excerpt from a work originally published by Ginn and Company in 1902. For the complete listing of the books that are published by Yesterday's Classics, please visit www.yesterdaysclassics.com. Yesterday's Classics is the publishing arm of the Baldwin Online Children's Literature Project which presents the complete text of hundreds of classic books for children at www.mainlesson.com.

ISBN-10: 1-59915-258-4
ISBN-13: 978-1-59915-258-5

Yesterday's Classics, LLC
PO Box 3418
Chapel Hill, NC 27515

CONTENTS

HOW THE TEUTONIC SEED
    OF SELF-GOVERNMENT PASSED
    FROM THE GERMAN WOODS
    INTO ENGLAND AND WAS
    FINALLY PLANTED IN AMERICA 1

HOW THE ART OF GREECE AND
    ROME WAS HANDED FORWARD
    TO WESTERN EUROPE THROUGH
    THE RENAISSANCE MOVEMENT......14

HOW THE REFORMATION CAME
    ABOUT, AND HOW IT
    INFLUENCED HISTORY IN
    EUROPE AND AMERICA 33

HOW THE TEUTONIC SEED OF SELF-GOVERNMENT PASSED FROM THE GERMAN WOODS INTO ENGLAND AND WAS FINALLY PLANTED IN AMERICA

THE stream of history is something like a river. The river rises often as a mere rivulet, but as it flows along, one tributary after another falling into it, first from one side, then from the other, it becomes wider and deeper, its current stronger, and its course continually more difficult to change.

We have now seen something of the early part of the stream and of the great men, cities and nations which grew up along its course. First arose great cities like Memphis and Babylon in the valleys of the Nile and the Tigro-Euphrates. Here man lived very simply. He was just working out an alphabet and the art of writing, and was making his first steps in literature, art, language, religion and government. Then as the stream flowed on westward, circling around the Mediterranean, the Phœnicians adopted the alphabet and the other useful things which the Old East had worked out, and through their trade scattered them around the Mediterranean coast as a farmer scatters seed on his fields. These things brought from the early nesting-places of civilization in the Orient furnished a foundation for the civilization of Greece, which thus by catching up the best ideas of the past, and adding to them her great ideas of literature, art and philosophy, made Athens the mistress of the Mediterranean. The stream then flowed on westward to the Italian peninsula. Here Rome, starting like a spider in the center of Italy, industriously spun its web out farther and farther till it caught and drew to its center all of the peoples living in the Mediterranean basin. From these people, and especially from the Greeks, Rome learned the lessons of art and literature and philosophy, but in turn taught them lessons of government, teaching them, however, not so much how to rule themselves, as how to be ruled by Rome. The imperial city became the center of the world, toward which every man, city and province looked as the giver of peace and order, and as the regulator of every detail of life. Thus Rome added to the great stream of human history *the idea of a strong central government*, giving out rules and laws to a vast empire, having a population, at its greatest, of perhaps one hundred and twenty million people.

But when the rude Teutons came through the passes of the Alps and gradually took possession of Rome, it looked for a time as if the stream of history was to be choked up and to flow no farther. It seemed as if the wealth and learning which had come down from the East, the art of Greece and the law of Rome, were all to be lost by the rude shocks of the uncivilized barbarian who at first seemed to care nothing for any of them. But slowly, and almost so noiselessly as not to be heard (except in time of intense persecution), the Christian missionary was opening up the channels through the Alps, so that the historical stream might flow northward from the Mediterranean into western and northwestern Europe.

Thus gradually through the monastery and the castle, and by the great movement of the Crusades and the Renaissance, were the channels opened so that all the great thoughts and ideas of the past might become the inheritance of the rude, uncultured children now ruling Europe. But these Teutons, who had spread as hunters, herders and fishers through the northern woods and valleys were not merely to have their lives enriched by coming to understand the great ideas of the past; they themselves, notwithstanding they were rude and barbarous at first, had also ideas which were greatly to advance the modern history of man.

The most important of these ideas was their strong love of individual freedom. When we were studying the early Germans in the previous volume of this series, we saw how intense was their love of liberty. Every man liked to rule himself, or at least to have an equal share with everybody else in electing the chief who was to rule him. He insisted on having an equal share in the public land, in the spoils gained in war, and when he built his villages he placed the huts so far apart that every one could have plenty of elbow room.

3

If the Teuton's love of individual liberty and local government as it was worked out in his "moot-court," could be preserved and added to Rome's great idea of a strong central government, then the modern European nations could build their foundations upon both ideas,—that is, they could have in the first place a strong central government to hold the people together and keep them in order, and keep off foreign enemies, and protect their commerce, and coin just one kind of money and the like; and yet, in the second place, they could have an active local government, which would allow the people to have their little meetings and assemblies near home where all could attend and take part in thinking out and making laws regulating their home affairs, such as dividing the land, pasturing the stock, building roads and the like. If both these ideas of government could be wisely united, a stronger and better kind of government than even Rome had developed, could be built up in the modern states.

Now there were many nations which finally sprang up, more or less, out of the Teutonic tribes. Spain, France, Germany, Italy and England were all growing to be strong nations, at the close of the fifteenth century,—that is, at the time Columbus discovered America. But among all these, there was but one single nation at this time that had, through many hard struggles and through hundreds of years, held firmly and constantly to the Teutonic idea of individual liberty, and the right of a man to rule himself, either directly or indirectly, by electing those who were to rule him.

This one nation was England. All the other great nations in Europe were slowly crushing the Teutonic spirit from their midst. This came about largely because the southern nations had sprung up on soil where the roots of the old Roman ideas of government were planted very deep and were therefore strong, and because these nations, living not so very far away from Rome, frequently thought of the great empire, and tried to build their governments upon the model worked out by Rome,—that is, upon the idea of a strong central government ruled arbitrarily by one man. Spain and France in particular had crushed out all thought of the Teutonic idea of local self-government, and in neither country at the time of the discovery of America were there regular assemblies or a parliament for making laws to which the people could go themselves or send their representatives.

But in England things grew very differently. Beginning in the fifth century (about 450) and continuing for six hundred years (1066, when William the Conqueror landed), swarm after swarm of Teutons invaded and settled in England. At first they went from northern Germany,—Angles, Saxons and Jutes,—and settling down in small groups, cleared a little land and divided it up just as they had done in the old German woods hundreds of years before. A few of the families living close together formed a township, and regulated their affairs in an assembly attended by all the freemen. Several of these townships, enough to furnish a hundred or so of warriors, formed what was called "The Hundred," which also had an assembly composed of representatives sent from the townships composing it.

5

Then as time went on and there came to be but one king in England, the little kingdoms of former days, such as those of the Angles, Saxons and Jutes, became shires, or, as we would say, counties. The county also, like the township and "The Hundred," had an assembly for attending to its affairs.

As already said, many companies of Teutonic people went to the rich and beautiful island. It was a little like an island of corn in a vast stream covered with river-fowl,—flock after flock would light, feed, build their nests and hatch their broods upon it. So the rich soil and mild climate of England invited settlers. After the first of the Angles, Saxons and Jutes had gone to England, almost continuous groups of the same people followed through the fifth, sixth and seventh centuries, each helping to plant more firmly Teutonic customs and institutions. Then in the eighth and ninth centuries the Danes came in, and in the eleventh century came the brave, free seamen who had learned on the waves of the Northern waters the lessons of courage, independence and self-reliance. These were called the Northmen, or Normans.

Before going into England, however, they had settled for a little time in northern France, and thus became acquainted with the language and culture of Rome, which, largely by means of the monastery and castle, had gradually spread itself through southern and central Europe.

These Normans, as they were now called, crossed the channel, under the leadership of William the Conqueror, and in 1066 conquered the island. But

6

they did not destroy or root up the Teutonic ideas of self-government which had been growing there for five or six hundred years before William's invasion of the island. But as soon as he had conquered the country, William did one thing which has been greatly to the advantage of England ever since,—he gave it a strong central government. He did not destroy the local governments which the Teutons so much liked, as the French and Spanish kings did in the centuries following this time, but he built up a strong central government in the midst of them, to keep them in balance and to protect them against both internal strife and foreign enemies. Thus England adopted both ideas—Roman and Teuton—as the foundation stones upon which to build her institutions. And the great difference between English history and the history of all other nations in Europe from the eleventh century down to the present time is, that England has been much of the time as fierce and as watchful as a tiger of its young, that no one should destroy either of these great principles of government; while other European nations have been content in the main to hold on to the idea of government as held by Rome.

But we must not think this Teutonic principle of self-government grew in England without great struggle. Time and time again, kings arose in England who would have been delighted to crush it out,—kings who would levy taxes without consent of the people, and spend the money on expensive wars or to keep up an expensive court.

One of the most arbitrary of these kings in early times, and one who cared least for the rights of the people, was King John. He was always needing money for one expensive thing after another, and always trying to get it by wringing it from the people in all kinds of oppressive ways. Finally the people, and especially the barons or lords, growing tired of this, armed themselves and went against John. The king tried to defend himself with an army, but nearly everybody deserted him, and he was compelled, in 1215 A.D., to sign an agreement with his people never to tax them again without their consent, never to imprison them without just cause, and to allow them to be tried by a jury when they were accused of wrong. This agreement is the most important document in English history, and is called Magna Charta, or the Great Charter. It is written on parchment, consists of sixty-three short chapters or articles, and is most carefully preserved in the British Museum in London.

The English people have never written a constitution all at one time and adopted it as their frame of government, as the United States did in 1787–1789; but from time to time they have written important documents and had their rulers assent to them, and these they regard as the foundation stones of their government and of their liberties. In English history there have been three of these very important documents:—

1. Magna Charta, secured in 1215.

2. The Petition of Right, passed by Parliament in 1628.

3. The Bill of Rights, passed by Parliament in 1689.

Among several other things, all these great documents declare the following great principles of liberty:—

1. No tax shall be levied upon any English subject without his consent.

2. No one shall be imprisoned without cause being shown.

3. When one is accused he shall have right of trial by jury.

Now, to work out these principles and to get them firmly established in the minds of the English people took a full thousand years or more—that is, from the first settlements of the Angles and Saxons and Jutes on the English coast, about 450 A.D., when they were planted in mere germ, down to 1689, when the English people brought them to much fuller fruitage by driving a very tyrannical king (James II) from the English throne and crowning William and Mary as king and queen on the condition that they would agree to the following principles:—

1. Not to dispense with any laws without consent of Parliament.

2. Not to raise any money except by consent of Parliament.

3. Not to keep a standing army without consent of Parliament.

4. To allow the people to bear arms without consent of Parliament.

5. To allow the people to petition the king.

6. To allow the freedom of debate in Parliament.

7. To allow frequent meetings of Parliament.

You see, from what the king and queen had to promise, they could do nothing except what they were allowed to do by the English people, expressing themselves through the great representative assembly called Parliament. And since the English Parliament has always been the greatest means by which the people have gained their rights and held on to their liberties, you must learn something about it.

Parliament comes from a French word, "parler," which means "to speak," and it was so called because the English people came together in this body to speak, or debate, about the best ways of carrying on the affairs of the nation. In Magna Charta, to which as you remember King John agreed in 1215, there was a provision that a council should be called to levy taxes whenever taxes were needed. The first council or parliament which was ever called of this kind in England was in 1265. It was called, not by the King himself, but by one of his subjects, Simon de Montfort, for the purpose of curbing the King's tyranny. To this parliament were summoned the few nobles who were in sympathy with De Montfort, representatives of the large landowners and representatives of the people living in the large towns. Thirty years after this time, in 1295, when a great English King, Edward I, was needing money to carry on war against the Welsh and the Scotch he assembled a Parliament, in which all of the classes of English people were represented, to ask them to vote him money.

In the first place there were summoned to this Parliament both the great nobles, such as dukes, earls and counts, and the great churchmen, such as bishops and archbishops. Then, since there were too many small landowners to come in person, there were two representatives chosen from each county to represent the general body. Next, from each city there were two representatives chosen. Next, from each burgh, or borough, or large town, two representatives were chosen. The representatives from the cities and towns represented the merchants and mechanics. Thus all classes of the English people were represented in the Parliament. It was the first time that this had occurred in England, or in the history of the world, and so important was it, in working out the liberties and greatness of England, that the great historian of the English people, John Richard Green, has called its assembling "the most important event in English history."

From this time forward Parliament grew step by step, sometimes having hard struggles when a king or queen sat on the throne who was disposed to rule without regard to the people's rights. But as the people grew in knowledge and self-reliance, their representatives in Parliament grew in courage, in love of liberty, and in willingness to risk their lives if necessary to keep those great Teutonic principles guaranteed by Magna Charta from being destroyed.

Now all of this long growth of liberty from the German forests up to England, and for ten centuries in

England, is of the greatest importance to us who live in the United States; for the germs and roots of the political liberties which we enjoy, as we have already seen, are buried deep in the history of our ancestors in England and our still older ancestors in the German forests.

When the New World was discovered, three great nations stood on the western coast of Europe and launched their ships toward the west,—Spain, France and England. The one which most fully represented all of the best and greatest principles of education, religion, government, industry and social freedom worked out by the world up to that time, would in all probability win the race in the struggle for the New World.

As already said, one of these nations only had been able to plant, nourish and develop in its political life the idea that every man should have the right to rule himself. England, by working out township and "hundred" and county assemblies, and by developing that greatest agent of liberty of the last five hundred years—the Parliament,—had given herself many centuries of schooling in self-government. This schooling had strengthened her people for the great undertakings in gaining wealth, culture, art, literature and free political life, which make England today as great as any nation on the earth. Hence when the English crossed the Atlantic in the seventeenth century and began to plant townships in New England, counties in Virginia, and legislatures in all of the colonies, she was sowing in the new soil ideas which had been ripening through many centuries in the old. And then later, when, at the time of our Revolutionary War, an arbitrary English king, George III, tried to stamp out this Teutonic love of self-government, it was the voice of Burke and Pitt in the English Parliament and of Samuel Adams and Otis and Patrick Henry in the legislative hall of the colonies and in the Stamp Act Congress (both the natural outgrowth of free Teutonic institutions) which did such great service in saving the principle of self-government for the whole English race—for England as well as America. Thus we see how old are the germs of the free institutions of our own country, and how impossible it would be for us to have them had it not been for our brave Teutonic-English ancestors who struggled to save and develop these liberties, hundreds of years before our country was discovered.

HOW THE ART OF GREECE AND ROME WAS HANDED FORWARD TO WESTERN EUROPE THROUGH THE RENAISSANCE MOVEMENT

1350–1550

THE first part of the word *renaissance* means *again*, and the second part means *to be born*. So the meaning of the whole word, renaissance, is, to be born again, or to spring up into new life. You have no doubt often watched the leaves come out in the springtime after the trees looked dead and bare for a long time during the winter months. These are not the same leaves as those that were there the year before. With the warm sun and early showers of spring, fresh sap has run up the body of the tree, and new leaves have been born. The renaissance was a period of time, extending through the fourteenth and fifteenth centuries, during which there was a new birth, of learning, in the minds of the European people. It was the European springtime which followed the Crusades, in which the old life of Greece and Rome blossomed out into great beauty, and gave a freer, richer life to the countries of western Europe, as we shall presently see.

You remember, in the study of the monastic life we saw that the monks copied a great deal, and that what they copied and recopied on those musty sheets of goat and calf skin was handed down to the people of later ages. You remember, too, that in the monastery were schools for boys. This shows that some persons were interested somewhat in learning. But the monastery was about the only place where there was any great interest in learning in those early days, and even the monks were frequently not greatly interested in the old writings which they spent a lifetime in copying. They copied sometimes because they were required to do so, and often for the sake merely of having something to do. People outside the monastery knew nothing of books, perhaps ninety-nine out of every hundred would have been unable to read the language which they spoke, and not one common man in a thousand could read Latin, which was the language in which the books were written. The monks generally knew nothing of the learning or literature of the Greeks, because they could not understand the Greek language, just as you and I today do not understand the literature of the Chinese or the Arabians, until some one translates it for us, because we do not understand their language.

We learned also in the second and third volumes of this series that the Greeks and Romans wrote a great deal, and that some of the very best thoughts of today have been handed down to us from the pens of those old scholars. Some of the greatest poets, painters, sculptors and philosophers that ever lived were to be found among the ancient Greeks and Romans, such as Homer and Virgil, Plato, Socrates and Phidias.

The flame of this brilliant civilization slowly died down, both in Greece and Rome, before those countries fell, but when the Germans, with their ignorance and spirit of conquest, went down and conquered Rome in the fifth century after Christ, it seemed that the flickering flame of culture would be wholly smothered out. But the monastery and the Mohammedan schools in Europe had kept sparks of it alive from 500 to 1400 A.D., and now in the fourteenth and fifteenth centuries it was to be fanned into a flame and to burst forth with a brighter light than ever. The stir that was set up in Europe by the Crusades resulted in a great increase in the activity of the minds of the people, and greatly broadened their knowledge. Colleges and schools began to rise, and men's minds began to long for greater freedom. They learned from visiting the universities of the Arabians that there were people in the world who were better educated than they, and had a hundredfold more of the comforts and luxuries of life. Stimulated by this, Europe began to shake off the torpor that had benumbed her mind, and to take on a more active life.

The greatest stir in this new thought first came about in Italy, partly because of the good position she held with regard to the commerce of the world; then like a river which gradually fills full of water to overflowing, the new stream of learning rose to such a height in Italy that, during the century in which Columbus lived, it flowed northward through the passes of the Alps and spread out over all western Europe.

This movement first began to show itself in the increased interest which men took in the literature of the Greeks and the Romans, and also in the study of nature. The men who were leaders in the movement were usually men of wealth and ease. They were thus able to travel and search for books themselves, as well as to employ others to search for them.

An Italian by the name of Petrarch was an early leader of the renaissance. He lived from 1304 to 1374. He felt the beauty of nature about him and had an intense desire to possess the writings of the whole ancient world. He wanted a broader view of life and the world than one could get shut up in a cell. It is said that he was the first man to climb a mountain for the mere pleasure of the journey and the delight of the scene from the top. He was a most enthusiastic collector of manuscripts and books and wrote some poetry. His father, wishing him to be a lawyer, had him spend much time in the libraries of the lawyers. Here he learned Latin, in which the law-books were written, but he studied very little law. He read with delight the writings of the old Latin poets and scholars. One day his father found a stack of books under the bed, and when he found that his son had been reading literature instead of law, he threw the books into the fire. The boy was so hurt by the unkindness of his father that he began to cry. The father then snatched a volume of Cicero and a volume of Virgil from the flames and gave them back to the boy. He grew up to be a great scholar, and the interest which his Latin writings

excited, his letters to friends and his enthusiastic studies caused other Italians to turn their attention to
the ancient classics. By the ancient classics is meant the
literature of the old Greeks and Romans. Petrarch influenced another great man of his time, Boccaccio, to
study Greek and to become a writer. He became one
of the greatest writers of the Renaissance period, and
like Petrarch greatly helped to spread among scholars a
love for the great writings of Greece and Rome. Students of the fifteenth century followed in their steps
and continued the collection of manuscripts. Some
traveled to Constantinople, to read in the libraries and
to learn Greek of the many excellent scholars who
lived and taught there. Some founded libraries at
home, and some lectured in universities. These men
were called humanists, by which is meant persons who
have great interest in all past human life of whatever
country or age, but more especially of the Greek and
Roman life.

Petrarch and Boccaccio lived much of the time
in Florence, which was the center of this new movement in learning. Florence is a city in northern Italy,
and at the beginning of the fifteenth century was the
wealthiest city in Europe. There were twenty-three
banks; many retail shops of silk and woolen goods;
workshops for artists in marble, gold and precious
stones; there were two hundred and seventy ware-
houses engaged in the woolen trade alone, and many
other thriving industries. This immense commerce
produced many rich families in Florence, who, when
they became wealthy, began to build fine churches,
public buildings, and costly palaces in which to live

and worship. In imitation of the Greeks and Romans they wished to make these buildings and the gardens and yards about them luxurious and beautiful, so they began to employ sculptors and painters who could make beautiful statues for the buildings and paint beautiful pictures upon the walls and ceilings of the palaces and cathedrals. This led a great number of men to turn their attention to the study of painting and sculpture. These artists naturally turned to the work of the old Greeks and Romans, and especially to the Greeks, to get their models, for, as we have learned, no people ever surpassed the Greeks as artists.

There lived in Florence at the beginning of the fifteenth century a very wealthy family known as the Medici family. They were bankers and carried on commerce with nearly all parts of the world. The members of this family were likewise great lovers of art. Thus their immense wealth and their artistic taste both together well fitted them for collecting manuscripts and specimens of art from all quarters of the earth. Wherever they found a rare manuscript or a fine piece of art, they had money with which to buy it. They built splendid palaces, fine libraries and gorgeous chapels. Lorenzo de' Medici, called Lorenzo the Magnificent, was greatly interested in art, and spent much time and money in collecting old manuscripts, pictures, statues and other relics, and in encouraging men to study art of all kinds. He lived about 1400 A.D., and many of those men who wished to study painting and sculpture went to his library. Some of the greatest painters that ever lived were first encouraged by him. Among these was Michael Angelo, who was as great a

lover of the sculpture of Greece as Petrarch and Boccaccio were of the literature. Michael Angelo is regarded as the greatest sculptor of modern times.

Another man who lived about the time of
Lorenzo and became intensely interested in collecting
books and old relics was Niccolo de' Niccoli. He was
the son of a merchant in Florence and inherited a
modest fortune. He gave up all business and devoted
himself entirely to the collection of manuscripts and
objects of art. He spent all he had in buying books and
sometimes even went in debt for more. He came to
have the best private library in Florence, having it is
said eight hundred manuscripts, which was regarded a
large library for that day. Many of these books were
very rare, being in some cases the only copies existing
in the world. Such copies were often worth vast sums
of money. Niccoli also had a small collection of gems,
statues, coins and pictures. He is said to have known
more about manuscripts than any other man of his
time. All the great men of his day wrote to him for information. He was much more generous with his library than most men of his time, being the first
collector who permitted his manuscripts to be copied
by others; and it is said that at his death there were two
hundred of his copies loaned out. His house was always open and was a sort of free school for scholars
and artists. At times there would be a dozen or so
young men quietly reading in the library, while he
would walk about the room, giving instruction or asking questions about what they read.

But Petrarch, Lorenzo and Niccoli were only
three of the many men who spent much time and

money in searching the world for manuscripts and relics of art. Men were hired to go in search of manuscripts, gems and specimens of ancient classical art, and there was no lack of men who were willing to go. These book-hunters and art-hunters ransacked the old monasteries from cellar to garret for the manuscripts of the monks. Some went to the temples of Greece, and others to the museums of Constantinople. As the Crusading Knights spent the twelfth and thirteenth centuries in trying to rescue the tomb of the Savior from unholy hands, and were thrice blest if they returned with relics from Jerusalem, so these Knights of the New Learning spent the fourteenth and fifteenth centuries in bringing from their musty tombs the remains of the great geniuses of Greece and Rome. Every corner of Europe and the East was ransacked for manuscripts, and whatever was found was purchased and brought back to Italy. Some of the manuscripts were brown with age, so old, indeed, that the writing on them was very dim. But no abbey, or monastery, or library, or museum was so far away, and no manuscripts so moldy, that these enthusiastic scholars did not joyfully search them out and feel repaid if, in years of quest, they could show for their labors some old copy of Cicero, or some ancient copies of the Greek poets and philosophers, which opened anew to them the delights and culture of the classical world.

Now, since they were so earnest in finding old manuscripts, you will be interested to know what they did with them when found. Some copied them on fresh pieces of paper, or parchment, bound them into books, and put them into their private libraries, while others made copies of books to sell to those of wealth and to the universities. Some men came after a while to own large libraries,—not what would be called large libraries today, but large for that time. Every book was written with pen and ink, for in the first part of the Renaissance time nothing was yet known of printing.

Students from other countries, who had caught the enthusiasm started by Petrarch, longed to have libraries of their own, so they came to the libraries of these Italian scholars and sometimes spent years in copying books. These copies they carried home with them. Think what labor and patience it cost a student in that day to get a valuable book, say Homer, or the Bible, as compared with the present time, when either may be had for fifty cents. So, at the beginning of this period of which we are studying, about 1400 A.D., could we have been in Italy, we might have seen men starting out in all directions from Florence, and from other centers of learning, generally on foot, to hunt for manuscripts and relics of art; others returning with a load of waxen tablets and musty sheets of parchment under their arms or strapped to their backs; others going empty handed toward Italy, to copy these manuscripts and carry them back home.

Thus, you see, the first work of the Renaissance was, in the main, to get together collections of ancient writings, and distribute them slowly to a few other scholars by means of copies made by hand.

But what was all this material worth if it could not be read? Most scholars in the early Renaissance period could read Latin, for the monasteries had taught Latin, and all books in western Europe were written in that language; but there were very few in western Europe at that time who could read Greek. How to read the Greek language, was the next question which they set about to answer. As already said, Petrarch induced Boccaccio to study Greek. This he did enthusiastically, but never became a good Greek scholar. Many others followed him, inspired by his example. One great difficulty was that they had no encyclopedias, dictionaries, or grammars as we have now, so you can imagine what a hard task they had when they began to interpret the Greek poets, philosophers and historians. The task was both a hard and a long one, but step by step Greek scholars began to appear in the West. Some students, in their enthusiasm, went to Greece to learn the language there, just as we would have to do today if the Greeks were the only people in the world who understood Greek, and there were no books to help us in the study of that language. When the Turks took Constantinople, in 1453, many Greeks went to Italy and carried with them Greek grammars, dictionaries and manuscripts. Some of these men were hired to teach literature in the schools and universities of Italy, while some traveled about from town to town, giving lectures upon Plato, Aristotle, Herodotus, Homer and others. Thousands of people eagerly listened to these lectures and took notes upon what they heard. In this way learning and the passion for the old classical life were diffused throughout Italy.

All this study produced, in the fifteenth century, a number of great scholars, who became experts in using the learned languages. These scholars began to sift and classify and explain the great mass of material which they had collected. They found many mistakes which had been made in copying, especially in the Latin writings produced in the monasteries during the most ignorant times of the Middle Ages. Many of the old books had been copied and recopied several times, and each time they were recopied new mistakes had crept in. Some of the monks were very careful in their copying, while others were just as careless. This led the scholars to say, "We'll go back to the original copy and find out just what the first writer actually said and thought about this or that thing." They thus began to compare the earliest manuscripts they could find with the later ones.

Thus they began to be critical and independent in their thought, and when this habit grew and spread it produced a great expansion and stir and independence in men's minds. The universities and lower schools, the church, the governments, science, art, literature,—everything began to feel that a new life was warming Europe and opening up new views, as truly as the sunshine opens the buds in the springtime. The old Greek thought was far freer and richer in many ways than the views which had been taught in the monastery during the Middle Ages. Some of these scholars began to study the governments under which they lived, and in some cases to criticise their tyranny and oppression. Others began to study nature, especially the stars and the motions of the earth, and to say that people had been taught wrong ideas about the universe. "The earth is round," they said, "instead of flat, and revolves around the sun instead of the sun revolving around it."

"The sun, and not the earth, is the center of the universe." These are a few of the most important things they began to think and say, and to be much criticised for saying, for it took a long while to get most people to believe them. Growing out of this new idea of the shape and motion of the earth was the courageous and self-reliant trip of Columbus across the Atlantic, in which he discovered the New World.

These students of Greek and Roman literature likewise began to study Hebrew literature found in the Bible, and to say, "Now here are certain traditions and ideas about religion that have been taught by religious teachers which we believe are not true. The teachers of the time have been studying copies of the Bible in which there were many mistakes. The only right method of gaining a true knowledge of Christianity is to go to the original sources of it." Thus in some cases they began to attack some of the teachings and practices of the church. Some of the monasteries had become hiding-places for immoral men, others had become places of idleness. Some of the monks and bishops had become corrupt and were not living simple, unselfish lives such as was the custom in the early Church. People were not allowed to worship freely in the way they thought best, as we can all do now, and they were required in many cases to pay a very high tax for the support of the Church. Those who were growing more independent began to criticise these practices quite fearlessly. One of the leaders, who made very witty and stinging criticisms, was an eminent scholar by the name of Erasmus. In his criticisms he did not spare kings, popes, or bishops, but spoke his mind very freely. About 1516 he made a Greek copy of the New Testament, and pointed out many errors in the Latin New Testament, which was the one used through the Middle Ages. Criticism of the traditions, doctrines and practices of the members of the Church, like these we have just spoken about, finally led some members of the Church to leave it and establish another branch of the Christian Church, called the Protestant, meaning by Protestant that they protested against the ideas and practices we have just been speaking about.

Thus far in our study of the Renaissance, we have seen that the libraries in Italy became beehives for scholars and artists, and that there grew up there many men who were skillful in the use of both the Greek and the Latin languages, and that many other persons were no less skilled in using the brush and the chisel. If we could have visited the palaces of one of those wealthy merchants, say Lorenzo the Magnificent, in the fifteenth century, we would have seen, in addition to the library, statues of marble in the splendid halls, the rarest paintings on the walls, carved furniture and the richest tapestries ornamenting the rooms; and the tables laden with rare porcelains, glassware and gold and silver plate.

How different from all this was the home of the plain, sturdy Teuton, who lived all his years on a little farm in some quiet valley or in a little hut on the mountain side. For a long time the happier, brighter life which the Renaissance was bringing to Europe did not touch his life. He had no books, no pictures, no statues to ornament his home, and in most cases only the chairs and furniture which he had rudely worked out by hand. How was he ever to get into touch with this new-blossoming life? How could the new learning which was coming to the palaces of the wealthy and well-born be given forth so that the cottages of the common people would become happier because the newer and freer thought had entered them. Just at the time when this new life was budding and many people were beginning to thirst for new knowledge, a means was invented for multiplying, cheapening and spreading it, so that everybody—rich and poor alike—might share in its uplifting influence.

About 1450 the printing press was invented, and this machine finally came to be the greatest means in modern times for spreading the new learning over the entire world. We learned in the earlier volumes of this series how the Egyptians wrote on stone and papyrus, the Babylonians on bricks, the Greeks and Romans on wax tablets and parchment, and the monks of the Middle Ages on parchment, or vellum. During the Crusades the Europeans learned from the Arabians how to make paper, so that, at the time the printing press came into use, paper was becoming plentiful. Paper soon became much cheaper than parchment, and by this means the poor as well as the rich came to have cheap writing-material. Not only this, but cheaper paper greatly encouraged printing, and with the printing press, when it was perfected, a thousand books could be made in the time which it had taken to make one when all the work was done by hand.

But we must not think that the printing press sprang into existence all at once. Like the steamboat, the telegraph, and all great inventions, it had its infancy, and it took many years for it to grow into the perfect and complex machine that it is today. If you would take a wooden block and with penknife carve your name upon it so that the letters would be raised, then smear ink over the letters and stamp your name upon a piece of paper, you would see what the printing press was like in its very beginnings.

The first printers had presses made entirely of wood, and as a rule printed but one page at a time. The wooden board into which the type were set, was fastened to the end of a wooden screw, which worked in a hole in the frame very much like the large screw works in a cider press. The sheets of paper upon which the printing was done were placed upon a flat, level surface underneath the board that held the type. Ink was then smeared over the type, after which the type was pressed down upon the paper by turning the screw in which was fastened a wooden handle. There were generally two men to one press, one who daubed two big soft balls, soaked with ink, over all the type, and another who placed the paper in place and turned the screw. We can easily see that when they had the type set for printing a page, they could print many pages in the same time that it took them to write a single one with pen and ink.

But the printing press was a long time in growing to a stage where it was of much use. It required careful and skillful workmen to prepare the type; and it was many years before men were able to make type smooth enough so that when they were set and ready for printing they would press down upon the paper alike. If one letter was a little longer than the others, a blot was sure to be made in printing. It was also quite a long time before an ink was invented that would work satisfactorily in printing. The chemistry which the Crusaders learned from the Arabs finally helped them to a successful ink.

When a machine that would print well was finally perfected, a whole book could be printed more quickly than a single page could be written by hand, and it was not long until printed copies of the old parchments, of the tablets, of the Bible, and criticisms upon these by great scholars, were scattered over all Europe. We can scarcely realize what a change this must have made; but suppose there were no books in our state except at the state capital and a few of the other large cities, and that if we wanted a copy, say of Robinson Crusoe, or the Bible, we should have to go to one of these towns and read it, or sit down with pen and ink and copy it, do you suppose that many people would have books? Certainly not. But with the invention of printing, things were greatly changed. The printing press meant that everybody could have books, and when everybody came to have them they began to want to learn how to read them. Thus universities were increased, and finally people in the most advanced countries began to build schoolhouses, where the children of all classes could go and learn to read. In fact the very schoolhouses in which we ourselves are studying, and the things we study in them, came to us largely through the Renaissance and the printing press.

Thus it came about that this culture and learning of which we have been speaking was no longer confined to a few universities and a few wealthy men, but began to be given out to all classes. This meant greater liberty of thought and speech and more abundant life for all. It meant a stronger national life for those nations which could take it up, for learning and culture are a strength and safeguard to the life of a people in even a truer sense than forts and armies are. An ignorant nation is likely to be a weak nation.

There was another thing which came into use in the middle of the fourteenth century, which did very much toward freeing the common people and preparing them to take advantage of the new thought and life of the Renaissance. This was gunpowder, which had been introduced into Europe from the East by the Crusaders. The use of gunpowder in firearms made it possible for the common people to fight on an equality with the nobility, since a peasant could handle a gun as well as a lord. Before gunpowder was used the great barons, being better armed, could, if they chose, go out among their neighbors, steal or plunder what they wanted, return and shut themselves in their strongly fortified castles, where they would be safe from all attacks. Men often tried to make machines with which to batter down the walls of the castle, but it required a great amount of work to make them, and when made they were very uncertain. When gunpowder came into use the peasants could stand off at a distance, and with cannon easily knock down the walls of the stately castle. The castle down, the peasant with a gun was able to defend himself from the lord and to demand greater justice from him.

Gunpowder also aided in producing in the lower and middle classes a number of people who had leisure, and who therefore could have time for studying the new literature and art which the Renaissance was producing. Before gunpowder was invented, during the feudal times, every man had to hold himself in readiness to go to war whenever his lord or king called upon him. When artillery came into use, it was found that a small army with firearms could accomplish as much as all the people formerly could with bows and arrows, especially if the small army were well drilled. Thus it came about that, instead of compelling every man to hold himself in readiness, each nation created a standing army,—that is, an army which was paid by the nation and was always kept in readiness for war. The standing army was also partly brought about by the fact that many men could not afford to buy guns when gunpowder came into use. Thus many of the common people were set free to look after their affairs at home and to accumulate wealth. Wealth led to leisure, and this in turn gradually gave an opportunity for many in all classes to take up the new learning, to build more comfortable homes, and to surround themselves with the beautiful and refining influences of ancient Greece and Rome, now spreading all over Europe by means of that greatest invention, perhaps, ever made by man,— the printing press.

Thus you see how, in the two hundred years from 1350 to 1550 A.D., the Teuton of southern Europe came fully to appreciate the rich inheritance left him by Greece and Rome; and having come to appreciate it, carried it forward from southern into northern and western Europe, and by means of university, printing press, book and, finally, newspaper, gave it out to the poor as well as to the rich. From this time forward, a nation, to be strong itself and to produce strong men able to compete with others, must give free development to these great agents of freedom. The nation which does this will have a continual re-birth (Renaissance) by the new life which flows into it; the nation that closes up these currents which bring new life will sicken, weaken and die.

HOW THE REFORMATION CAME ABOUT, AND HOW IT INFLUENCED HISTORY IN EUROPE AND AMERICA

1550–1650 A.D.

THE word Reformation comes from two Latin words, "formare," meaning to form, and "re," again. Thus the word means to form again. Now we wish to see what was formed again, or made over, and where it was done, and when.

You have already seen how the Renaissance woke up southern Europe from her slumber, and set the scholars hunting up old books and writing new ones; and how, before the Renaissance, the Crusades brought new life to commerce, and made Europe and Asia, join hands by means of great trade routes which extended from one end of the Mediterranean to the other. Now, just as broader ideas were coming to the minds of men in trade and learning, so also were many persons getting finer and fresher ideas about religion; and these new ideas led to new life in the Christian Church, or Catholic Church, as it was then called, since its ideal was to spread Christianity over the entire world.

The period when the idea of reforming the Church took hold of the people so deeply that they talked and struggled for it more than for any other one thing was the sixteenth century; that is, the century just following the discovery of America. But we must keep our minds free from thinking that the Reformation sprang up all at once, as a mushroom springs up, so to speak, during the night. Instead of this, everything which helped to open the minds of people to new thought for four or five centuries before the sixteenth was a step which led, either directly or indirectly, to the Reformation. Let us very briefly review these steps and see how they lead to this one common point.

First, during the twelfth and thirteenth centuries came the Crusades; and these two hundred years of travel between Europe and Asia wonderfully opened the eyes and minds of the travelers, as travel generally does; then came, as a result of acquaintance with the lands around the Mediterranean, a passionate love for the old literature—especially for Greek and Latin literature; this began in the fourteenth century, and no manuscript was too musty, or dim, or too hard to read, to keep the scholars from cleaning the dust off of it and reading it; thus the springs of Greek and Roman thought began to flow again and refresh the minds of western Europe; then, right in the middle of the Renaissance movement (1453), the barbaric Turks, in moving westward from Asia, conquered Constantinople, which had been for a thousand years the storehouse of much of the old Greek writing. This drove the scholars westward, but as they went they carried with them their precious manuscripts as a miser would his gold; thus was Europe further enriched by what the old times had to teach, and thousands of scholars began to study the history, the literature, the philosophy and the art of old Greece and Rome; then, as we have already seen, printing was invented about 1445, which opened the doors to a higher and finer life to common people, as the universities had opened new realms of thought to the well-born. Then came the difficulty about paper, for the materials out of which paper was made, and especially parchment, had grown so scarce and costly that the price of books was as high as ever; but with the invention of linen paper, about 1300, and the immediate growth thereafter of the paper-making trade, the cost of books was greatly reduced, which made it possible for more people to have them.

You might think now that with the printing press and cheap paper secured, all the people would have books and be able to read and study them. But you must remember that the books were written mostly in Greek and Latin, and that not many at this time could read Latin, while very few indeed could read Greek. To overcome this difficulty, learned scholars who could read these languages gathered at the great university centers which had grown up in Europe mainly during the fourteenth and fifteenth centuries, and began to teach the Greek and Latin languages and literature to the scholars who could come to them. So, notwithstanding the fact that the great mass of the people could not read the ancient classics, and only a few, comparatively, could go to the universities, yet what was discussed there was more fully and freely discussed than it had been in the monastic schools, and as these new ideas slowly trickled down among the people, the great mass gradually came to know and think about them, and catch glimpses of a freer life.

It was the custom too, in that day, for the scholars to pass from one university to another, spending say a year or so in Oxford in England, then another in Paris or Orleans in France, thence on to Prague or Heidelberg in Germany, and then on to Padua or some other great university in Italy. In this way the new thought which was taught at any one university would soon be scattered more or less all over Europe.

Some of the earliest scholars who attended several of the great universities lived in England. They studied first at Oxford and then went to Italy, where the opportunity was especially good for learning Greek and Latin. John Colet was one of these scholars. He was the son of a lord mayor of London and inherited a fortune from his father; but after studying much in Italy, he returned to England and spent his life and fortune in trying to give his country a simple Christianity based on the Golden Rule, and also a better opportunity for the common people to educate themselves. He established a school in London for boys, taught it himself, and even wrote the text-books which the children studied.

Thomas More was another great scholar of the time. He especially helped on the movement toward freer thought by writing a book, "Utopia," in which he described the manners and customs of an ideal country: in this country the people should elect their own officers, make their own laws, carry on very little war, all be able to read and write, and all be well off instead of having the wealth in the hands of kings, princes and lords, as was the case to a great extent in all European countries at that time.

Still another very learned scholar was Erasmus, whom we learned something about when studying the Renaissance. He was an orphan and poor. In youth he had been placed in a monastery by his guardians, but when he came of age he left the monastery, and by giving lessons to private pupils gained the means to secure an excellent education at the University of Paris; then he went to Oxford and became a fellow-pupil of Colet and More, possessing with them a passionate love for Greek, Latin and the literature of the Romans and Greeks. But he, like others, was not satisfied till he had traveled to Italy and studied under the great teachers who taught there. While he was in Italy he was near Rome,—the very head of the Church,—and observed how worldly many of its officers had become, the way they mixed themselves up with political matters, and gave their time to striving for power, pleasure and money. A man as learned as Erasmus was sure to hate such trifling with religious matters as he saw in many of the clergy, and as he rode back through Europe from Italy toward England on horseback, he devised a plan for rebuking them for their trifling and vice. When he came to his old friend, Thomas More, in London, he stopped for a time before going on to Cambridge University, where he was to teach Greek. In More's house he wrote a book, "The Praise of

Folly," in which he very wittily ridiculed teachers and preachers who knew but little but pretended to know everything. He described monks as shut out of heaven because they had grown to be trifling and lazy; and he even criticised the Pope, Julius II, by saying that instead of "leaving all" as St. Peter did, he was trying by war and conquest to add continually to St. Peter's possessions. This book, which was, perhaps, sometimes too severe in what it said about both monks and popes, was printed and sold broadcast, and many people opened their eyes to the weak spots Erasmus pointed out, and began to laugh at the follies which he held up to ridicule.

Then Erasmus went on to Cambridge University, and for years taught and studied Greek, till he wrote a book which did more than any other one thing to give new and fresh thought to his time. This was the New Testament, containing in two columns, side by side, the original Greek and a new Latin translation of his own. He was thus able to place before the people a picture of the daily life of Christ and His Apostles in all the freshness of the original language. This book was much studied at the universities, and presently it was translated into the language of the common people, and thus they came to have a Bible which they could read as well as the clergy. "I wish," Erasmus said, in his preface to his New Testament, "that even the weakest woman should read the Gospels—should read the Epistles of Paul; and I wish they were translated into all languages, so that they might be read and understood not only by Scots and Irishmen, but also by Turks and Saracens. I long that the husbandman should sing portions of them to himself as he follows the plow; that the weaver should hum them to the tune of his shuttle; that the traveler should beguile with their stories the tedium of his journey."

Thus you see, by travel, books, printing, cheap paper, and universities where thousands of young, ambitious scholars gathered for discussion and study, Europe was being sown with germs of new thought. Old things in philosophy, literature, government and religion were no longer believed by the most thoughtful simply because they were old; many were examining the old theories of religion, government and education, and wishing to push forward to newer truths and broader views.

But just as the Bible speaks of the sower who sowed seed on different kinds of soil, some producing abundant harvest and others none at all, so the seeds of new thought scattered over Europe in the first part of the sixteenth century, and especially new thought on religion, sprang up in some countries rapidly and in others it was choked out.

Let us now see how it grew in different places. There was one country where the soil was in many ways just ready to receive the seed of independent thought. This was Germany. Perhaps if you could have seen the people in that country, you would have wondered how this could be. The Germans who lived in the cities were well off and had many comforts and privileges. The peasants on the farms, however, were generally downtrodden and half-fed, to say nothing of comforts and rights. The central government was very

weak, Germany being still cut up by the feudal possessions of numerous lords. Thus the peasants had no
one to appeal to when they were oppressed. They were
obliged to work for the lords without pay except the
miserable living which they obtained from the land. At
the end of the year the feudal lord took the best of the
crops and cattle; the Church a tithe of all they produced, that is, a tenth of the grain, every tenth calf, pig,
chicken, egg, etc. Being naturally a vigorous, healthy
race of people, living in a bracing climate, and, as we
saw earlier, naturally disposed to free life, the Germans
grew tired of being oppressed, and were ready for the
new ideas that were now being spread abroad. It is but
natural, then, that the greatest reformer of all this time
should come from the people who were great lovers of
freedom, and who, though they had been crushed by a
thousand years of Feudalism, still had in mind ideas of
personal liberty which if they could have a leader
would burst forth with great power.

This great leader of the time in religious matters
was Martin Luther. His great-grandfather and grandfa-
ther were Saxon peasants. His father was a miner.
Thus he sprang from the common people and his early
life was spent amid very lowly conditions.

He was nine years old when Columbus set sail
across the Atlantic, being fifteen years younger than
Erasmus. His early home training was very severe, and
his school life while a boy was stern and hard. Although not a bad boy, he was often whipped at school.

His first home was at Eisleben, a mining town
in Saxony, but his parents afterward moved to Magde-

burg, a town about seventy-five miles southwest of Berlin, and Luther attended school there. After staying a year at Magdeburg, he went to Eisenach, another neighboring town, to study. Here he studied reading, writing, arithmetic and music. His parents being poor, it became necessary for Luther to make his own way at school. He partly did this by singing on the streets. His beautiful tenor voice and polite manners made warm friends for him; and making his own way only taught him that self-reliance which served him so well in his great battles in after life. He did so well in his studies that his father determined to make him a lawyer, and by great economy sent him to Erfurt University, one of the old universities in central Germany. Here he studied philosophy, Greek and Latin, and became one of the best students there.

Some time before graduating, a trifling thing happened which changed the whole course of his life. One day he found a Latin Bible while looking through some of the university books. It was the first Bible he had ever seen, and with the greatest delight he read the pages again and again. He was surprised to find how much there was in it; for in the religious services which he had gone through with from childhood in the monastery he had heard only the meager quotations of the monks. To get the whole Bible and read the chapters and books through in connection, was to him like reading a wholly new book. He began to think about what he read, and a new world of religious life slowly dawned upon him.

Luther, as I have already said, was reared among peasant people, who were superstitious; and he there-

fore naturally inherited some superstitious ideas himself, some of which clung to him to the end of life.
When he was twenty-three years old, in fulfillment,
some say, of a vow made during a dreadful thunder-
storm, when he thought his life was near an end, he
gave up his law studies and entered a monastery at Erfurt. Here he obeyed most faithfully the rules of the
monastery, fasting and praying much, and sometimes
shutting himself up in his cell for days; once he was
found senseless on the floor of his cell, so greatly had
he been stirred up by his religious thoughts and practices. But all of these things did not bring him peace of
mind. When he was twenty-five years old he was called
as a preacher and teacher of the Bible to Wittenberg, a
new university in northern Germany. He was still
greatly troubled by religious thoughts, and very rigidly
practiced fasts, penances and ceremonies of the
Church, but without getting quiet of mind. Finally,
while explaining the Epistle of St. Paul to the students
of the university, new light came to him in a passage
which gave him great peace. It was this: "The just shall
live by faith." It meant to him that forgiveness of sins
was not to be obtained by ceremonies, penances and
fasts, but would be given freely by Christ to all who
had faith in Him, and lived daily as Christ lived. He
thought if one were truly sorry for sin, he would be
pardoned then and there by God; and that, therefore,
outward fasts, penances and confessions were not so
important as some officers of the Church were claim-
ing. Full of this new thought, and with his heart full of
new hope for the Church, Luther set out for Rome in
1510, when he was twenty-seven years old, on an er-
rand for his monastery. While there he found, just as

Erasmus had, many religious practices which gave his high ideals a great shock. The rites and ceremonies which were being performed in the churches by worldly men, and the pleasure, idleness and ease of many in the Church, made Luther's hot nature burn with anger; and he left Rome to return home, feeling that he must and would go to the Church and peasants in the Fatherland and preach to them a higher and finer life.

Now it would be very far from the truth if you should think that all officers and members of the Church were, at this time, lovers of wealth and pleasure, and cared nothing for the simple religion of love for one another and love to God, which was taught by Christ and His Apostles. There had been in every age of the Church before this time many noble popes, thousands of capable bishops, and legions of saintly monks and nuns. Thus from about 400 to 1100 A.D. the rude Teutonic children were taught the lessons of kindness, gentleness and brotherhood by monk and nun; great popes, such for example as Gregory VII (1015–1085), loved right and hated wrong so intensely, and gave their great powers so completely to reforming the abuses of their times, and to keeping high-minded men as leaders and preachers in the Church, that not only their own time, but all aftertime, has felt the benefit of their noble influence. St. Francis of Assisi (1182–1226) was so gentle in life and word, and so pure in soul, that when the Church became careless in his day, millions forsook their wayward leaders and leaped to follow in the footsteps of this beautiful-souled Saint. But by the time of the sixteenth century the membership of the Church had grown to be less pure than at some other times; and even such great scholars as More, Colet and Erasmus criticised both kings and popes, when they saw how the common people were oppressed and deceived.

After Luther returned home he continued for several years in his duties in the university, teaching, and working for the reform of the Church by preaching in the towns around Wittenberg, but never dreaming of leaving it. Finally, in 1517, Tetzel, a Dominican monk and seller of indulgences, appeared in the neighborhood of Wittenberg. The Pope, Leo X, was very desirous of obtaining money, to complete St. Peter's, a very large and beautiful church in Rome; and in order to get this money, "he offered to grant indulgences, or pardons, at a certain price to those who would contribute money to the building of St. Peter's." Thus there came to be at this time agents who were traveling from place to place selling pardon-certificates, or "indulgences."

Many of the most intelligent people in the Church opposed what Tetzel was doing, but others, especially the more ignorant, and those greatly desiring money, said pardon for sins might be obtained in this way. When Tetzel appeared near Wittenberg, Luther was greatly stirred.

As we have seen, Luther was one of the common people; and as he loved and sympathized with them, he did not like to see them imposed upon. Besides, he knew that the sale of indulgences, as then carried on, instead of making true Christians, encouraged false and formal worship. For this reason he determined to put a stop "to selling pardons for sin," as he called it. If Luther had lived in our time, he might have written an article on the evils of selling pardons and had it printed in the newspapers. But there were no newspapers at that time; so he wrote ninety-five statements against the sale of indulgences, and on the day before the festival of All Saints, when the relics of the Church were shown and all the country people flocked into town, he nailed them to the door of "All Saints Chapel" in Wittenberg, where everybody could read them. Notwithstanding the lack of newspapers, all Europe, and especially the people of northern Germany, soon heard of this and became much excited over it; for, to speak so boldly about what was being done by the head of the Church was not common. Soon Luther was challenged to a discussion with Eck, an old fellow-student, and one who supported Tetzel and others in selling the "pardon certificates." This was held at Leipsic, about twenty-five miles south of Wittenberg.

The discussion was held in the open air, on a platform, in order to accommodate the crowd. Luther was very fearless in his discussion. He said that he thought God was the author of good, and not the Church; that the Pope had no power to forgive sins, that God only could do so; and that the sale of indulgences was corrupting the Church and the people and should be stopped.

If these had been simply Luther's views and nobody had paid any attention to them, the Pope would have cared very little for them; but as discussions went on, and pamphlets were published by the printing press and eagerly read, many people came to think as Luther did. Soon Leo X became alarmed at the spread of the new thought, and in 1520 sent a written statement to Frederick of Saxony (the ruler of the country in which Luther lived), saying that Luther was preaching false religious doctrines, that he was therefore a heretic. The Pope then wrote a statement ordering Frederick to give Luther up, so that he might be taken to Rome and tried for heresy. This was called a Papal Bull.

What will Frederick do with Luther, and what will Luther do with the Bull?

Frederick had the interests of his people much at heart; and as he believed that Luther was largely right on the main points, he would not give him up.

As to the Bull, when it arrived in Wittenberg, in December, 1520, Luther was teaching in the university there. He formed a solemn procession of his fellow-professors and the students of the university, marched through the principal street of the city, through the gate leading out of the walls to a market place, and there amid cheers burned the Bull and some Roman law-books. He burnt the Bull to declare his individual right to whatever religion he thought best. He burnt the Roman law-books to declare that Germany was from that time to be ruled by the law of the land and not by the law of Rome. Luther said that if there had been a mountain at Wittenberg he would have lit his bonfire at the top, and let the whole world see the Pope's Bull ablaze in its flames.

Luther, in his earnestness and hot temper, said harsh things, and especially attacked persons in the Church in language which was not always respectful and just, and which his best friends regretted; but such defiance and boldness as he showed could not help but attract the thought of all Europe to what he said and did, and especially did his name and fame increase rapidly in Germany.

While this was going on, those who opposed Luther were busy thinking what should be the next step taken to crush his ideas. Germany at this time was loosely ruled over by an Emperor, and a body of men somewhat similar to our United States Congress, called a Diet. This Diet, about two hundred in number, was composed of representatives of the nobles, the highest German officials of the Church, and of representatives of the greatest German cities. The Diet met annually at different cities to hold their meetings and the emperor presided. Charles V, a very powerful ruler, was at this time emperor, and he decided to call Luther before the Diet of Worms (so-called because it met at Worms, in southern Germany) and have him admit that what he had said was heresy and wrong.

This meeting was called in 1521, and the emperor of Germany sent orders to Luther to appear before it and answer for his writings. The journey from Luther's home at Wittenberg to Worms was about two hundred and fifty miles. In the dress of a monk, and amid the tears of his friends, many of whom did not expect him to return alive, he with three companions and a herald, who rode ahead with a trumpet, started in a covered farm-wagon on a fourteen days' journey to Worms. Throughout the trip throngs of people followed him, and although he was ill during a part of the time, he is said to have preached with such eloquence as moved many of his hearers to tears. Those who flocked to the towns to hear him were the peasant people of Germany, who in their downtrodden condition felt the warm heart of their great leader as the "plain people" in our own country felt the leadership and sympathy of our great common man—Lincoln.

On arriving in Worms, Luther was summoned before the Diet. There were about two hundred members of the Diet present, and in addition, five thousand spectators who had gathered in and around the hall. The emperor himself presided. Luther's books were piled up on a table before him, and he was asked to admit that they were heretical, and to retract what was said in them. Luther's enemies expected him to reply in a rage, but his conduct was modest. He frankly admitted that he wrote the books, and asked the Diet to give him until the next day to say whether he would retract what was in them. That night he wrote to a friend.

"With Christ's help I will never retract one tittle." At four o'clock the next day the officers came to bring him before the Diet again. The streets were full of people, and spectators climbed to the tops of the houses to see him as he was led through passages and private ways to escape the crowd. As he walked up the crowded hall some said an encouraging word or shook his hand, and a sympathizing prince said to him, "Little monk, you have a great work before you!" Then he took his place at the table, where his books were piled. Around him were princes, nobles and kings. The great representatives of the Church were there. The emperor of Germany, Charles V, the most powerful ruler then in Europe, was there to preside. It was as if all royal and ecclesiastical Europe were there, looking scornfully upon this peasant preacher who dared to say that religion should be chiefly a matter between the individual and God rather than outward forms and symbols of worship, and that one's conscience should be free in choosing whatever religion he thought best.

Then Luther stood up and heard the one question which Europe had gathered there to ask, "Martin Luther, do you retract those books or not?" Then came the answer: "Before I can retract I must be convinced either by the testimony of the Scriptures or clear arguments that I am wrong. . . . I am bound by the Scriptures which I have quoted; my conscience is submissive to the word of God; therefore I may not, and will not recant, because *to act against conscience is unholy and unsafe.* So help me God! Amen."

Several other efforts were made in the next day or so to have him retract, but all in vain. He stood bravely and fought the battle for that free thought which so many of his nation were hungering for. And he fought it not only for his own people, but for all Christendom, of whatever creed, for the discussion which he brought about on such great questions as the nature of sin, repentance, forgiveness, faith, prayer, and what is required to live truly as Christ lived while on earth, has influenced the thought of the last four hundred years perhaps more than any other one thing occurring in that time.

The emperor now ordered him to leave Worms and return home. The hero now of the German people, he set out again for home, but his friends, fearing that he might be seized by his enemies and put to death, secretly carried him off to the castle of the Wartburg in Thuringia, where he remained in the disguise of a gentleman for a time, letting his beard grow, wearing a sword at his side, dressing like a knight, and being known to all except intimate friends as Junker George. But all this time he was watching the growth of thought among his countrymen and preparing the greatest gift he ever gave to the German people. This was the Bible, which he translated with great care from the Latin into such pure German that the Germans still today, three centuries and a half after Luther, speak and write it just as Luther wrote it in his Bible and hymns.

After this, and by means of the printing press, all the people of his country could have a Bible in their own language. Luther's translation was intended to be simple and to reproduce the tone and spirit of the original texts. He said he wished "the Bible to be understood by the mother in the house, by the children in the streets and by the common man in the market." It was completed in 1522, and became at once the household book throughout northern Germany.

Now came another effort to destroy the influence of Luther; after Luther would not retract at Worms what he had written, the Pope asked Charles V (who, you remember, was king of Spain and emperor of Germany) to order all Luther's books burnt. So Charles sent a letter, or Edict, as it was called, to all parts of his empire, ordering this done. In some places they were, but the people burnt Charles's Edict in more places than they did Luther's books. And so the Reformation of the Church rapidly grew in Germany.

We will not follow Luther year by year through the remainder of his life. He continued writing books as long as he lived, writing in all more than a hundred. He labored most diligently to increase learning and spread it out among the people. He constantly and eloquently advocated free thought and free speech, but he did not always practice his principles toward others as fully as he advocated them. He was sometimes ruled by superstition, and thought that persons could, at times, see devils and be possessed by them. Toward those who differed from him in opinion he often used harsh, violent, coarse and even shocking language. But with all his many faults, it can truthfully be said that as he gained greater knowledge he became more just and gentle toward his fellow-men. As his horizon of thought widened he more frankly and frequently confessed his errors; and when he was taunted with being inconsistent (and in fact he frequently was so) he said "I thought so once; I was wrong. I think so no more. I appeal from Luther in ignorance to Luther well informed,"—and this is not a bad habit to follow for one who is earnestly seeking the truth.

Luther believed that monks should marry; that by having homes and families of their own they would be better men. He therefore married and reared a family, being kind, amiable and cheerful in his own family circle, and, amid the most heated discussions and conflicts, which often called him from home, wrote the most tender letters to "Kate," as he called his wife, and to "little Johnny," as he affectionately called their son.

He died in 1546, in his sixty-third year. By advocating and practicing to a degree the principle that one should have the right of free worship, and by starting all Christendom to practicing this principle, so that it now follows it much more wisely than it did then, Luther became the greatest man of his nation, the greatest of his time, and one of the greatest men of any nation and of any time.

During the quarter of a century between the Diet of Worms and Luther's death there was very earnest discussion of religion in Germany. As I have already told you, Germany was divided into many little feudal states, at the head of each being a prince. Some of these princes sided with Luther and others with the Pope, so Germany finally came to be divided into two great opposing camps on the subject of religion. Those who sided with Luther went on rapidly in the work of reform. Monasteries were reformed or torn down and the money used for education, for supporting the preaching of the Gospel, or for the poor. Monks and nuns were allowed to marry; religious services were generally carried on in German rather than Latin. The children were taught in the common schools, and Luther's German Bible and German hymns came into general use. It thus came about that centers of new thought in education, in government and religion sprang up in almost the whole of northern Germany— that part which was most Teutonic and had been least influenced by Rome—and laid the foundation for the sturdy, independent people who have made Germany in our day one of the greatest nations in the world.

During the sixteenth century other European countries were also stirred with these same questions of reform. In Spain reformers arose who translated the Bible into Spanish for the common people, and strove for free religious thought.

But so much were the Spanish king and the leading authorities in the Church opposed to all this, that they appointed a body of men to inquire carefully into every person's religious opinions; and if they were not such as the Church wished them to have and they would not retract, they were either tortured or burnt. Inquiring into the religious opinions of people, and punishing those who did not believe and practice what the Church wished, was what is called the Inquisition. The story of the treatment of reformers in Spain is more cruel than that in any other country. And so perfectly did the Inquisition do its work in that country that it plucked up all roots of the new thought which were springing up there. And just as Germany has grown wealthier and stronger by continually taking up new thought during the past four hundred years, Spain has grown weaker and poorer by crushing all new thought out of her country.

In France, at this time, as in Spain, there was one powerful ruler at the head of the government, who ruled his people practically without consulting them at all. This ruler, in the time of Luther, was much opposed to the thought of the reformers, or Protestants, as they were now generally called. But notwithstanding this, a reformer who has had almost as great an influence on the world as Luther was born in France at this time and educated in her great universities of Paris and Orleans. This was John Calvin. He was twenty-five years younger than Luther. He was born in 1509. By the time he became of age, he was considered a heretic by the Church, and as heretics were burnt in France at that time he left home to travel in Germany and Italy. While he was still a young man he settled in Geneva, Switzerland, and became a powerful advocate of the new doctrines there. He thought that every congregation should have the right to choose its own preacher, just as the Baptists, Presbyterians, Congregationalists, for example, do nowadays. He thought that the preacher and congregation had the right to make people go to church, go to school, give up swearing, dancing, playing at dice, etc. He ruled after this manner in Geneva the greater part of his life, strongly advocating religious freedom, and, like Luther, writing many books upon it; but also, like Luther, sometimes failing to practice it (for he had one man, Servetus, burned with his books hung to his girdle, for an honest difference of opinion from him on religious matters).

But notwithstanding his faults, he was a man of great ability, and his better ideas were caught up in France by reformers who called themselves Huguenots, and at first they grew very rapidly. During the sixteenth and the first of the seventeenth centuries the Huguenots came to be, so far as industry, education and moral character were concerned, the foremost people of the French nation. But as I have already told you, the French rulers were opposed to the Huguenots. One ruler in 1572 had twenty thousand—some say one hundred thousand—massacred in one fatal night. Finally, in 1685, after much bloody struggle between Huguenots and Catholics, Louis XIV had all the Huguenots banished from France. France thus cut off her right arm, so to speak, for in banishing the Huguenots she banished industry, free thought, and manly independence. Some of the Huguenots went to England; others came to the American colonies, and were the forefathers of men like John Jay, Henry Laurens who did so much for liberty in the early history of our nation, and Peter Faneuil who built "the cradle of American liberty," as Faneuil Hall, in Boston, has been called. Thus, you see, when the Huguenots were not allowed to enjoy freedom in the Old World, they came to the New and struggled all the more bravely to establish liberty in America.

Holland and Denmark, as you will see by the map, lie just north of Germany, and Sweden is not so very far away. In all these countries the lamp of the new truth was lit by the reformers in the sixteenth century, and all rapidly developed independent Protestant churches of their own. Especially did little Holland become a home to which the oppressed of all nations could flee and enjoy the fullest degree of religious liberty. You remember the Pilgrim Fathers, who braved the seas to plant the spirit of the Reformation in New England, went from England to Holland when they were no longer allowed to worship freely in their native land.

Let us now notice very briefly how the new ideas of religious reform grew in England.

England was in one way like, and in another way very different at this time from Germany. She was like, in being occupied by freedom-loving Teutons, who were always jealously guarding their liberties; she was unlike in having a single king instead of petty princes who ruled over the entire country. Now the King of England could not rule just as he pleased, but had to ask the people through their representatives in Parliament what they wanted done. The king ruling in England while Luther was preaching and working so earnestly in Germany was Henry VIII (1509–1547).

Henry VIII at first did all he could to help the Pope destroy Luther's ideas, but something occurred to make him change his mind. He had married his brother's widow, Catherine, the daughter of Ferdinand and Isabella of Spain. Catherine was older than he and in poor health, and, besides, he had fallen in love with a young and handsome woman named Anne Boleyn. Henry asked the Pope to grant him a divorce from Catherine, saying that he thought it wrong for one to marry his brother's widow, as the Bible forbids this in the eighteenth chapter of Leviticus. But the Pope very properly refused to grant the divorce. At that time one could not get a divorce from courts as is done sometimes now. The only possible way was to get it from the Church. What was Henry VIII to do?

He conceived the plan of leaving the Catholic Church entirely, of setting up a new Church in England where the spirit of religious freedom had already grown considerably, and of getting Parliament to declare him the head of it. If this were done, he knew he could secure the divorce through Parliament without consulting the Pope. This was accomplished in a few years, and Parliament declared Henry VIII "Supreme Head of the Church of England." This is generally said to be the beginning of the Episcopal Church, or Church of England, and from this sprang the Church in America known as the Protestant Episcopal Church.

Henry's reason for leaving the Catholic Church was selfish and ignoble, but from his leaving it, sprang up thereafter true reformers, and great principles of religious freedom developed, because of what he did, in both England and America. We will mention some of the great steps by which this came about.

One of the first steps toward reform taken by Henry after he was declared head of the Church was to shut up a part of the monasteries in England, of which there were at that time over six hundred.

The monks and nuns had lived very simple, sacrificing and useful lives in early times, when they were showing by example the heathen of western Europe the kindness and love of Jesus and His Apostles; but in a thousand years of growth the monasteries had become wealthy, and many monks and nuns were living idle, useless lives; and instead of practicing true religion, they often did little more than keep up its forms and ceremonies. By being idle and ignorant some also became immoral. So Henry, partly through greed (because he wanted the property of the religious houses to use in war and for his own pleasure), shut up a part of them, turned the monks and nuns out into the world, pensioning some, and using some of the money obtained from the monasteries in establishing schools and colleges. The schools and colleges would become freer as they became less controlled by the Church, and people of all religions would have a better chance for education than they had had before.

A second very important step taken by Henry was to order an English translation of the Bible made and put in all the churches, that people might read it. This translation was begun by Tyndale in 1525 and was continued by English scholars till it was completed nearly a hundred years later (in 1611). A copy of the new translation was kept chained to the reading-desk in every church, and the common people who were too poor to own one themselves joined together and purchased a neighborhood Bible. Henry thought that by teaching every one to read the Bible and use the prayer-book, people would learn to pray for the king and others in authority instead of the Pope. They did learn to do so, but they also learned to think freely on religious subjects, and this habit finally led them to set up religions without asking leave of either king or Pope.

A third very great step which helped on the Reformation in England was the effort made by Elizabeth, Henry VIII's daughter (who ruled during the last half of the sixteenth century, 1558–1603), to have everybody in England worship alike. She got Parliament to say that Catholic and Protestant should meet together and use the same prayer-book, recite the same creed, and use nothing but the English language in the Church service. There were now getting to be many in the Church who, more in earnest and much more sincerely than Henry, objected to some of the Church doctrines and ceremonies. For example, many did not like to see the surplice worn in the pulpit, as it reminded them of the preachers before the Reformation and practices and beliefs of earlier centuries. They did not like to see pictures of saints in the church, for much the same reason. These people wanted to purify the English Church by having the preacher leave off the surplice and many other forms and ceremonies then practiced, and hence they came to be called Puritans.

When the law was passed compelling them all to attend church whether they wished to or not, many Protestants went to Germany, Holland and Switzerland, where they became all the more filled with ideas of reform, and especially with John Calvin's ideas, which taught that people have a right to set up little congregations, and worship God just as they see fit, without asking permission of any one. They became so filled with this idea that when England would not let them practice it at home, they willingly left their friends, kindred and country, to come across the sea and plant the new idea in the New World.

Thus when the Pilgrim Fathers and the people of Boston settled on the New England shore, they brought with them the very ripest and choicest seed of the Reformation to plant in the new soil.

This germ of liberty has grown in our land till it has given the greatest freedom to everybody— Catholic, Protestant, Jew and pagan—to worship as his conscience tells him is right, so long as his worship does not interfere with the rights of others. And so precious is this to us, and cost so much struggle to obtain, that when our fathers came to write our national Constitution they said expressly and definitely that Congress shall make no law favoring one religion more than another, or any law to prevent one from having whatever religion he wishes.

To sum up, we have now seen in studying the Reformation that it was:—

First, an effort made to place the Bible in simple and plain language before the people that they might thus be able to decide religious questions freely for themselves, and take whatever steps seemed to them best in following the teachings and life of Jesus and His Disciples.

Second, that this led reformers to translate and print thousands of books and tracts so that common people could read them. And these gave the people excellent models of speech in their own tongues—English, French, Dutch, and German,—which led to the writing of many new books and to the development of a great literature in each of these countries.

Third, it led the great religious teachers to establish schools for teaching their religious ideas,—schools were established by Calvin in Geneva; by Savonarola in Florence; by Edward VI in England; by John Knox in Scotland; by Ignatius Loyola over almost the whole world, and by the Puritans who settled in Massachusetts. These schools rapidly grew in numbers and in free thought, and soon came to teach the new ideas of science which were now springing up in the minds of great men like Copernicus and Galileo, as well as the new and freer ideas of religion and government.

Fourth, it led to the destruction of many of the monasteries which had lost their higher life, and made people believe that married life is as sacred and exalted for religious leaders as the unmarried; and that for modern times the public school, open to every shade of thought, offers a better opportunity for training the mind to broad and liberal views than schools over-shadowed by the Church.

Fifth, we have seen that the Romance countries—Spain and France—crushed out the plants of free religious thought, and have been ever since weaker therefrom; while the Teutonic countries—England, Germany, Holland, Norway and Sweden, cultivated the seeds till they took firm root in the Old World and spread to the New.

Sixth, we have seen that the growth of free ideas was so strong in England that, when it was checked there for a time in the first quarter of the seventeenth century, those who would not suffer the lamp of liberty to be quenched left home and friends, crossed stormy seas, and planted the hard-won principles in free schools, free religions, free labor (in the North) and free government up and down the Atlantic seacoast from Maine to Georgia during the seventeenth and eighteenth centuries. And it is this idea of individual liberty and self-reliance which has cleared the forest and built the Republic from the Atlantic to the Pacific during the nineteenth century, and now rules and molds the life of the New World.

But the chief result to us in studying the Reformation should be to lead us away from narrow and intolerant religious views. We should not think that the Catholic was all wrong in his opinions and the Protestant all right, nor the Protestant all wrong and the Catholic all right. It would be a better view to see that no human mind and no Church can at any time possess the whole of truth; for truth, as grasped by man, is continually growing. All churches in order to grow, therefore, must be continually gaining higher and truer views. But truth grows most rapidly by every one having a chance to tell freely the way he sees it; it was, therefore, a great gain that the Reformation of the sixteenth century brought about *a freer discussion of religious matters* than had ever existed before, and this freer discussion in turn has brought about, in the four hundred years since the Reformation, vastly better *means* of discussion and education, such as the printing press, books, magazines, newspapers and pictures. Thus we may see that, although at first every religion, because of the intense earnestness, and ability of its followers to see but one side of the question, was intolerant of every other, the distant fruit of the Reformation has been that it has broadened the views of all branches of the Christian Church, made all more earnest seekers after the Truth, made every one more willing to consider and tolerate views—religious, political or social—which may differ from his own, and helped all mankind, of whatever sect or creed, to see that every age and every branch of the Universal Church has had, and in order to grow must continue to have, its mighty teachers and reformers standing like guide-posts, pointing mankind to a higher, freer and finer life.

CPSIA information can be obtained
at www.ICGtesting.com
Printed in the USA
LVOW03s0043221117
557265LV00001B/131/P